I0159164

PETER MAURIN'S

ECOLOGICAL LAY NEW MONASTICISM

A Catholic Green Revolution Developing
Rural Ecovillages, Urban Houses of Hospitality,
& Eco-Universities for a New Civilization

JOE HOLLAND

Pacem in Terris Press Monograph Series

PACEM IN TERRIS PRESS

Devoted to the memory of Saint John XXIII,
Founder of Postmodern Catholic Social Teaching,
and in support of a Postmodern Ecological Global Civilization
and a Postmodern Ecological World Church

www.paceminterrispress.net

Copyright © 2015 Joe Holland
All Rights Reserved

ISBN-13: 978-0692522806
ISBN-10: 0692522808

PACEM IN TERRIS PRESS
is the publishing arm of the
PACEM IN TERRIS GLOBAL LEADERSHIP INITIATIVE.
*The Initiative calls for an authentically postmodern human and Christian renaissance
that will be holistically artistic, intellectual, and spiritual,
and that will serve the global regeneration of ecological, social, and spiritual life.
The Initiative is sponsored by*

PAX ROMANA
Catholic Movement for Intellectual & Cultural Affairs
USA
*1025 Connecticut Avenue NW, Suite 1000
Washington DC 20036
www.pax-romana-cmica-usa.org*

Dedicated to
my visionary and inspiring friend
MABEL GIL
who grew up close to the Catholic Worker community
as playmate and companion of Tamar, daughter of Dorothy Day,
Both Mabel and Tamar were tutored by Peter Maurin
Now in her nineties, Mabel still speaks with love's prophetic voice

Doomsday predictions can no longer be met with irony or distain. We may well be leaving to coming generations debris, desolation, and filth. The pace of consumption, waste, and environmental change has so stretched the planet's capacity that our contemporary lifestyle, unsustainable as it is, can only precipitate catastrophes ... The effects of the present imbalance can only be reduced by our decisive action, here and now.

FRANCIS OF ROME
Laudato Si' - On Care for Our Common Hope

The Catholic Worker
is taking monasticism out of the monastery ...
The aim of the Catholic worker
is to create a new society within the shell of the old,
with a philosophy of the new
which is not a new philosophy but a very old philosophy,
a philosophy so old that it looks new.

PETER MAURIN
Easy Essays

TABLE OF CONTENTS

Preface   1

Peter Maurin's Prophetic Vision   3

    Alasdair MacIntyre's Call for a New Monasticism   3

    Peter Maurin's Vision of a New Monasticism   4

    Three-Point Program of Peter's Green Revolution   6

    The Unemployed Planting Seeds of a New Society   10

    Beyond the End of the Modern World   13

    Summary of Peter's Vision   14

Appendix 1: About Peter Maurin   17

Appendix 2: Washington Declaration   25

Books from Pacem in Terris Press   31

Additional Books by Joe Holland   33

About the Author   34

PREFACE

This monograph about the radical-traditional prophetic vision of Peter Maurin (1887-1949), co-founder with Dorothy Day of the Catholic Worker Movement, is an edited excerpt from a book of mine forthcoming from Pacem in Terris Press. It carries the lengthy title TOWARD THE DAWN OF POSTMODERN CATHOLIC ECOLOGICAL SPIRITUALITY: *The Twilight of Modern Psychological Spirituality, the Dark Night of Modern Industrial-Colonial Civilization, & Peter Maurin's Call for a New Lay Monasticism.*

That book is the first in a series of three books that I am writing for Pacem in Terris Press. The series explores the ecological, social, and spiritual breakdown of Modern Industrial-Colonial Civilization. (Originally Western, that civilization is now revealing its breakdown across the planet in the form of neo-liberal globalization.) The series also explores the seeds of a postmodern global civilization, which needs to be electronic and ecological, and to seek guidance from the deep philosophical and spiritual wisdom traditions of the entire human family.

That first book traces the spiritual and philosophical side of breakdown. It does so by reviewing the history of Western spirituality up to the "twilight" of its modern psychological form. It then points to the "dawn" of a lay ecological spirituality, and finds a creative resource in the "new monasticism" called for by Peter Maurin.

1

The second book carries the title SOCIAL ANALYSIS II – END OF THE MODERN WORLD: *Toward an Authentically Postmodern Global Electronic-Ecological Civilization*. It will explore more closely the social and ecological dimensions of the modern breakdown and point us toward a new global civilization.

The third book carries the title REMEMBERING THE PROPHETIC VISION OF SAINT JOHN XXIII: *Radical-Traditional Founder of Postmodern Global-Ecological Catholic Social Teaching*. It will explore John's global and ecological stage of Catholic Social Teaching as a creative response to the postmodern transition.

The above three books provide foundational background for the Pacem in Terris Global Leadership Initiative. The Initiative calls for an authentically postmodern global human and Christian renaissance to support the regeneration of ecological, social, and spiritual life across our Creator's beloved garden-planet Earth.

The Pacem in Terris Global Leadership Initiative also sponsors three projects, two of which are already up and running. Those first two are Pacem in Terris Press, which is publishing the above books, and the Pacem in Terris Ecovillages Project. This monograph, explaining Peter Maurin's lay ecological monastic vision, is published in support of the Ecovillages Project. The third project will be an intellectual center for research and education.

Alasdair MacIntyre's Call for
a New Monasticism

At the end of the first edition of his profound book AFTER VIRTUE, philosopher Alasdair Macintyre – a Scottish former Marxist turned Aristotelian and later Catholic Thomist – prophetically called for a new yet different Saint Benedict.

> [For] our own age in Europe and North America and the epoch in which the Roman empire declined into the Dark Ages ... certain parallels are there ... This time however the barbarians are not waiting beyond the frontiers; they have already been governing us for some time ... We are waiting not for Godot, but for another – doubtless very different – St. Benedict.[1]

Later, in his Prologue to the Third Edition of that book, MacIntyre continued his theme.

> Benedict's greatness lay in making possible a quite new kind of institution, that of the monastery of prayer, learning, and labor, in which and around which communities could not only survive, but flourish in a period of social and cultural darkness ... Ours too is a time of waiting for new and unpredict-

---

[1] Alasdair Macintyre, AFTER VIRTUE: A STUDY OF MORAL THEORY, Third Edition (University of Notre Dame Press, 2007), p. 263.

able possibilities of renewal. It is also a time for resisting as
prudently and courageously and justly and temperately as
possible the dominant social, economic, and political order of
advanced modernity [2]

Macintyre's call has become an important part of the wider call
for, and experiments in, a "new monasticism."

I describe this "new monasticism" in more complicated fashion
as an *authentically postmodern lay monasticism of ecological, social,*
and spiritual regeneration. Yet, while there are abundant experiments in various forms of the "new monasticism," this monograph is not the place to investigate them, nor to delve more
deeply into Macintyre's philosophical analysis.

Peter Maurin's Vision of
a New Monasticism

This monograph presents for study the prophetic, radical, and
paradoxically traditional vision of Peter Maurin.[3] Peter's vision
stands as an authentically postmodern prophetic call for a Catholic lay "new monasticism" of ecological, social, and spiritual regeneration, with the adjective "ecological" also serving as a com-
prehensive metaphor for the entire process.

Within the contemporary ecological, social, and spiritual breakdown of Modern Western Industrial-Colonial Civilization, now
expanding across the planet as the late modern financial empire

---

[2] AFTER VIRTUE, p. xvi.

[3] On the life and "green" teachings of Peter Maurin, see Dorothy Day and Francis
J. Sicius, PETER MAURIN: APOSTLE TO THE WORLD (Orbis Books, 2004). On the
Catholic Worker movement, see *www.catholicworker.org.*

of neo-liberal "globalization." In response to this breakdown, Peter's vision of planting seeds for a "new society" calls to us today even more powerfully than when he first proclaimed it.

Peter understood his prophetic vision as a contemporary reenactment of the seventh-century work by Irish missionary monks who, after the collapse of the Western Roman Empire, evangelized the migrating 'barbarian' tribes and laid the intellectual-spiritual foundation for regenerating Western Civilization.

Writing during the Great Depression of the 1930's and referring to the collapse of "modern empires," Peter called for planting creative seeds of what I now call (in somewhat cumbersome fashion) an authentically Postmodern Global Electronic-Ecological Civilization.[4] At the same time, Peter implicitly called for planting creative seeds of a postmodern ecological "New Evangelization."

---

[4] Note that I see this new global civilization as based technologically on the Electronic Revolution. There have been some in the Catholic Worker Movement, however, who tend to reject technological advances as foreign to Peter's vision. Yet that assumption is incorrect, for Peter embraced the printing press (at the time a massive technology) and arranged for phonographic recordings of his "Easy Essays." (Thanks to Dr. Francis J. Sicius, for this information.) Such critics of technology within the Catholic Worker appear to have been guided by the famous work of Jacques Ellul, THE TECHNOLOGICAL SOCIETY (Vintage Books, 1967). Ellul offered a powerful critique of Modernity's enslaving technological utilitarianism. Yet technology need not be limited to its modern philosophical-scientific reductionism. Indeed, the Greek word *techne* means "art." There can be destructive art and creative art. Fossil-fuel technologies, for example, when employed as the basic energy system of a society, become destructive art. Renewable energy systems, however, can become creative art. Certainly, Peter – with his embrace of the printing press and phonographic recordings, as well as his constant use of trains and buses – was not fundamentally anti-technological.

Three-Point Program of Peter's
Green Revolution

Overall, Peter named his program the *"Green Revolution."* Its three-point practical program included what he called *"rural communes"*[5] and urban *"houses of hospitality,"* with both linked to what he called *"agronomic universities."*

Today, we might describe Peter's program of "rural communes" as a Catholic expression of the global movement creating "ecological villages," or more simply *"ecovillages."*[6] We might also describe his Catholic vision of "agronomic universities" as "agroecological universities"[7] or "ecological universities," or more simply as *"eco-universities."*

Again in today's language, we might reframe the *three points of Peter's program* for this "new monasticism" as follows:

---

[5] On the growing development of Catholic Worker "rural communes," see Eric Anglada, "The History and New Growth of Catholic Worker Farms," AMERICA MAGAZINE, May 6, 2013, available at: *http://americamagazine.org/issue/taking-root.* On one moving example, the "Peter Maurin Farm" managed by Tom and Monica Cornell (two long-time Catholic Worker members), see "Farmer Sees Fresh Catholic Worker Energy," NATIONAL CATHOLIC REPORTER, 9 Nov. 2013, at: *http://ncronline.org/news/peace-justice/farmer-sees-fresh-catholic-worker-energy.*

[6] On the ecovillage movement around the world, see the website of Global Ecovillage Network at *www.gen.ecovillage.org.* See also Hildur Jackson & Karen Svensson, ECOVILLAGE LIVING: RESTORING THE EARTH AND HER PEOPLE (UIT Cambridge, 2002) and Diana Leafe Christian, CREATING A LIFE TOGETHER: PRACTICAL TOOLS TO GROW ECOVILLAGES AND INTENTIONAL COMMUNITIES (New Society Publishers, 2003).

[7] On the concept of Agroecology, see *www.agroecology.org,* as well as Miguel A. Altieri, AGROECOLOGY: THE SCIENCE OF SUSTAINABLE AGRICULTURE, Second Edition (Westview Press, 1995).

1. *Rural Ecovillages,* planting seeds for a post-capitalist and post-Marxist ecological society, yet one with ancient communitarian roots in rural bioregions;

2. *Urban Houses of Hospitality,* ministering to people marginalized by the 'progressive' breakdown of Modern Industrial-Colonial Civilization;

3. *Integrating Eco-universities,* seeking intellectual clarification for the historical transition to the new society.

Again, Peter described his three-part program as a re-enactment of the Irish monastic evangelization of the migrating 'barbarian' tribes after the collapse of the Western Roman Empire. In the free verse of his "Easy Essays," Peter wrote the following description of his program. (Note that, in quotations from Peter's "Easy Essays," I have placed his main points in bold font.)

> *When the barbarians invaded*
> *the decaying Roman Empire,*
> *Irish missionaries went all over Europe*
> *and laid the foundations of medieval Europe.*
>
> *Through the establishment of* **cultural centers,**
> *that is to say,* **Round-Table Discussions,**
> *they brought thought to the people.*
>
> *Through* **free guest houses,**
> *that is to say,* **Houses of Hospitality,**
> *they popularized the divine virtue of charity.*
>
> *Through* **farming colonies,**
> *that is to say,* **Agronomic Universities,**
> *they emphasized voluntary poverty.*

It was on the basis of
personal charity and voluntary poverty
that Irish missionaries
laid the foundations of the social order.[8]

Describing his program in another essay, Peter wrote of "bringing thought to the people" by establishing "Centers of Thought." In describing the intellectual work of the early medieval Irish monks, Peter (once a member of a Catholic religious order) preferred in lay fashion to call them "scholars."

*When the Irish **scholars***
decided to lay the foundations
of medieval Europe,
they established:

Centers of Thought
in all the cities of Europe
as far as Constantinople,
where people could look for thought
so they could have light;

Houses of Hospitality
where Christian Charity was exemplified;

Agricultural Centers
where they combined:

(a) **Cult** *– that is to say,* **Liturgy**
(b) *with* **Culture** *– that is to say,* **Literature**
(c) *with* **Cultivation** *– that is to say,* **Agriculture.**[9]

---

[8] Peter Maurin, EASY ESSAYS (Franciscan Herald Press, 1961, 1977, 1984), p. 17.
[9] EASY ESSAYS, p. 142.

Again drawing on medieval resources and writing about the "people who built the Cathedral of Chartres," Peter linked the third part of his program, "Culture," with "Philosophy."

> *People who built the Cathedral of Chartres*
> *knew how to combine*
> *cult, that is to say Liturgy*
> *with culture, that is to say **Philosophy**,*
> *and cultivation, that is to say Agriculture.*[10]

In yet another essay, Peter called his program the "*Catholic Workers' School.*"[11]

> *The program of the **Catholic Worker School***
> *is a three-point program:*
>
> 1. *Round-table Discussions*
> 2. *Houses of Hospitality*
> 3. ***Farming Communes** [i.e., farming villages]* [12]

Having grown up in France where the word "commune" means "village," Peter in his third point was referring to the creation of *farming villages*, which had been implicitly ecological from time immemorial.[13]

---

[10] EASY ESSAYS, p. 28.

[11] EASY ESSAYS, p. 36.

[12] EASY ESSAYS, p. 36.

[13] In an interview with Arthur Sheehan, Peter clearly identified these "communes as "villages." Referring to the U.S. homesteading movement, he stated that "here in America people ... forgot the village idea, which was in Europe, but went off by themselves." In addition, although Peter wrote in his "Easy Essays" constantly of "thought," "scholars," and universities, in this interview he spoke of "folk

9

The Unemployed Planting Seeds
for a New Society

In these farming villages, Peter called for integration of scholarship and labor, with both aimed at creating a "new society, and linked scholarship and labor with the unemployed.

> *We need Communes*
> *to help the unemployed*
> *to help themselves.*
>
> *We need Communes*
> *to make **scholars out of workers***
> *and **workers out of scholars** ...*
> *We need Communes*
> *to create **a new society***
> *Within the shell of the old.*[14]

Again, writing during the Great Depression of the 1930's, Peter especially emphasized the unemployment of college graduates, whom he presumably viewed as future leaders.

---

schools where children would learn folk dances and folk songs." Hence, for Peter the folk-art dimension was to be an important part of his vision." The interview was printed serially in the CATHOLIC WORKER, July, May, June, and July-August, 1943. (Thanks again to Dr. Francis J. Sicius for bringing this interview to my attention.)

[14] EASY ESSAYS, pp. 36-37. During the time when Peter was writing, there was a Catholic movement to re-create ecovillages. See Dr. Tobias Lanz et al., FLEE TO THE FIELDS: THE FOUNDING OF THE CATHOLIC LAND MOVEMENT (IHS Press, 2003). See also Fr. Vincent McNabb, THE CHURCH AND THE LAND (IHS Press, 2003), originally published in 1925.

On Farming Communes
unemployed college graduates
will be taught
how to build their houses,
how to gather their fuel,
how to raise their food,
how to make their furniture;
that is to say, how to employ themselves ...
[They] will learn to use
both their hands and their heads.[15]

In calling for this "new society" Peter anticipated what may be called the still developing postmodern global and ecological stage of Catholic Social Teaching.

Decades later launching that new stage with his two great encyclical letters MATER ET MAGISTRA (1961) and PACEM IN TERRIS (1963), Saint John XXIII would officially reject modern ideologies and call globally for "a new social order."

Similarly, Saint John Paul II constantly wrote of moving beyond modern ideologies, and especially in his great 1981 encyclical LABOREM EXERCENS.

More recently, Francis of Rome in his great 2015 encyclical LAUDATO SI' also rejected modern ideologies and called for "ecological spirituality," for "ecological education," and for a "bold cultural revolution."

---

[15] EASY ESSAYS, pp. 92-93.

Decades earlier rejecting modern ideologies, Peter wrote:

> *The Catholic social philosophy*
> *is the philosophy of the Common Good ...*
> *Christianity has nothing to do*
> *with either modern capitalism or modern communism ...*
>
> *The capitalists, or accumulators of labor,*
> *[treat labor] not as a gift, but as a commodity ...*
> *But the buyers of labor ...*
> *are nothing but commercializers of labor ...*
>
> *[Further] as some people used to think*
> *that we need a good honest war to end all wars,*
> *Karl Marx used to think*
> *that we need a gigantic class-struggle*
> *to bring about a classless society.*[16]

Instead of the "Bolshevik Red Revolution," Peter – again ahead of his time – called for a "*Green Revolution.*" Implicitly ecological, his Green Revolution was intended to bring people back to the land. Thus, he wrote:

> *The only way to prevent a Red Revolution*
> *is to promote a **Green Revolution.***
> *... to make them look up*
> *to Green Ireland of the seventh century.*[17]

---

[16] Easy Essays, pp. 37, 15, 31.

[17] EASY ESSAYS, p. 71.

Beyond the
End of the Modern World

Quoting a Father Gillis,[18] Peter said that his three-point program was necessary because "this age is very much like the age of the fall of Rome."[19] He thus linked the contemporary late modern Western period with the ancient fall of the Western Roman Empire.

In so doing, Peter anticipated what the mid-twentieth century Italian-German Catholic philosopher Romano Guardini would later call the "End of the Modern World,"[20] Yet in this dire situation, Peter lamented, "Catholic bishops have failed to lead."[21] He also despaired of finding leadership from "college professors or "universities, including "Catholic professors" and "Catholic colleges."[22]

In his own creative response to the "End of the Modern World," Peter once again argued that we need to repeat the program of the "Irish scholars" of the seventh century.

---

[18] James Martin Gillis, CSP, was a Catholic Paulist priest who from 1922-1948 served as Editor the Paulist review CATHOLIC WORLD. During that time, he became one of the most publically known Catholic priests in the United States.

[19] EASY ESSAYS, p. 12.

[20] That is the English translation of the title of Guardini's 1950 masterwork, DAS ENDE DER NEUZEIT , 9TH edition (Wűrtzburg, 1965). See also the English translation, THE END OF THE MODERN WORLD (ISI Books, 1998). Pope Francis, while still a young Jesuit, worked on a doctoral dissertation about Guardini. Later, in his great 2015 ecology encyclical LAUDATO SI', Francis cited Guardini's book *eight times*! Peter reportedly read Guardini's earlier writings.

[21] EASY ESSAYS, p. 21.

[22] EASY ESSAYS, p. 23, 26-27, 53, 59, 86, 90.

In order to lay the foundations of medieval Europe,
*the Irish scholars established **Salons de Culture**.*

In all the cities of Europe as far as Constantinople,
*the Irish scholars established **free guest houses**.*

*The Irish scholars established **agricultural centers***
all over Europe ...

What was done by Irish missionaries
after the fall of the Roman Empire
can be done today
*during and after the fall of **modern empires**.*[23]

Summary of Peter's Vision

Peter proposed a radical, prophetic, yet traditional "green" vision of regenerating the human family's millennia-old experiences of living in ecovillages ("farming communes"). He linked that tradition with welcoming marginalized people ("houses of hospitality"), and with intellectual regeneration.

In the intellectual search for a "new society," Peter centered his regenerative vision in an Earth-rooted intellectual process of scholarship and teaching ("cultural centers," "round-table discussions," "salons de culture," "centers of thought," and "agronomic universities"). Again, for that intellectual task, he especially drew on Catholic Social Teaching.

Finally, Peter integrated his vision of regenerative education with a revival of small-scale agriculture and the arts and crafts, as well as with folk music and folk dance. In addition, he sought

---

[23] EASY ESSAYS, pp. 205-206.

the integration of work-life and intellectual life. ("Workers will become scholars and scholars will become workers.")

Today, at the "End of the Modern World," can contemporary visionary pioneers integrate postmodern electronic technologies with Peter's radical, traditional, and regenerative three-point program?

Can contemporary visionary pioneers plant humble and authentically postmodern seeds for regenerating the creative communion of ecological, social, and spiritual life across our loving Creator's beloved garden-planet Earth?

Can contemporary visionary pioneers thus create healing ecological, social, and spiritual alternatives to the late modern ecological, social, and spiritual devastation?

APPENDIX 1

The following narrative about Peter's life and work is the article titled
"Peter Maurin" as found in WIKIPEDIA, *the free encyclopedia.*
The original references have been omitted here,
and they may be found in the original article at:
https://en.wikipedia.org/wiki/Peter_Maurin.

ABOUT PETER MAURIN

Note. As may be clear from some of the books that Peter recommended
(listed later in this article), he rejected the regulatory state and state-
sponsored social-insurance programs, as well as modern labor unions.
In taking such positions, however, Peter was rejecting key elements of
orthodox Catholic Social Teaching. Even so, there is no reason why the
heart of Peter's vision (what I have called rural ecovillages, urban
houses of hospitality, and eco-universities) could not be combined with
orthodox Catholic Social Teaching.

P eter Maurin (May 9, 1877 – May 15, 1949) was a Catholic social activist who founded the Catholic Worker Movement in 1933 with Dorothy Day. Maurin expressed his ideas through short pieces of verse that became known as Easy Essays.

Biography

He was born Aristide Pierre Maurin into a poor farming family in the village of Oultet in the Languedoc region of southern France, where he was one of 24 children. After spending time in the De La Salle Brothers, Maurin served in the Sillon movement of Marc Sangnier until he became discouraged by the Sillonist shift from personalist action towards political action. He briefly moved to Saskatchewan to try his hand at homesteading, but was discouraged by the death of his partner in a hunting accident. He then traveled throughout the American east for a few years, and eventually settled in New York.

[About Peter's vision, Dorothy Day wrote on the centenary of his birth:]

> *Round-table Discussions, Houses of Hospitality and Farming Communes – those were the three planks in Peter Maurin's platform. There are still Houses of Hospitality, each autonomous but inspired by Peter, each trying to follow Peter's principles. And there are farms, all different but all starting with the idea of the personalist and communitarian revolution ... Peter was not disappointed in his life's work. He had given everything he had and he asked for nothing, least of all for success.*

For a ten-year period, Maurin was not a practicing Catholic "because I was not living as a Catholic should."

In the mid-1920s, Maurin was working as a French tutor in the New York suburbs. It was at this time Maurin experienced a religious conversion. He was inspired by the life of Francis of Assisi. He ceased charging for his lessons and asked only that students give any sum they thought appropriate. This was likely prompted by reading about St. Francis, who viewed labor as a gift to the greater community, not a mode of self-promotion. During this portion of his life, he began composing the poetry that would later be called his Easy Essays.

Dorothy Day and the Catholic Worker

"Peter Maurin first met Dorothy Day in December, 1932." She had just returned from Washington, D.C., where she had covered the Hunger March for COMMONWEAL and AMERICA magazines. At the Basilica of the National Shrine of the Immaculate Conception on December 8, 1932, the feast of the Immaculate Conception, Day had prayed for inspiration for her future work. She came back to her New York apartment to find Maurin awaiting her in the kitchen. "He had read some of her articles and had been told by George Schuster, editor of Commonweal, to look her up and exchange ideas with her."

For four months after their first meeting, Maurin "indoctrinated" her, sharing ideas, synopses of books and articles, and analyzing all facets of daily life through the lens of his intellectual system. He suggested she start a newspaper, since she was a trained journalist, to "bring the best of Catholic thought to the man in the street in the language of the man in the street". Maurin initially proposed the name CATHOLIC RADICAL for the paper that was distributed as the CATHOLIC WORKER beginning May 1, 1933, during the depths of the Great Depression.

His ideas served as the inspiration for the creation of "houses of hospitality" for the poor, for the agrarian endeavors of the Catholic Worker farms, and the regular "roundtable discussions for the clarification of thought" that began taking place shortly after the publication of the first issue of The Catholic Worker.

Maurin at times saw the paper as not quite radical enough, as it had an emphasis on political and union activity. Shortly after the paper's first print run in early May, 1933, he left New York for the boys' camp at Mt. Tremper, where he worked in exchange for living quarters. "[T]he paper, declaring its solidarity with labor and its intention of fighting social injustice, was not, by Maurin's standards, a personalist newspaper." Maurin believed the Catholic Worker should stress life in small agricultural communities. As he liked to say, "there is no unemployment on the land."

Maurin lived for much of [the rest of] his life in Easton, Pennsylvania, where he worked on the first Catholic Worker-owned farming commune, Mary Farm. He also took part in the Catholic Worker picketing of the Mexican and German consulates during the 1930s.

Maurin traveled extensively, lecturing at parishes, colleges, and meetings across the country, often in coordination with the speaking tours of Dorothy Day. He addressed venues as varied as Harvard students and small parishes, the Knights of Columbus, and gatherings of bishops and priests.

Later Years

In 1944, Maurin began to lose his memory. His condition deteriorated until he died at the Catholic Worker's Mary Farm near Newburgh, New York, on May 15, 1949, "the Feast of St. Dymphna, patroness of mental health, the anniversary also of St. John Baptiste de la Salle, and the Papal encyclicals RERUM NOVARUM and QUADRAGESIMO ANNO ... Many remarked on the strange convergence of anniversaries." At the wake, many people were seen to touch their rosaries to his hands surreptitiously, indicating their belief in his sanctity. The Staten Island Catholic Worker farm was named after Maurin following his death; it currently operates in Marlboro, New York.

Intellectual System

Maurin's vision to transform the social order consisted of three main ideas:

- Establishing urban houses of hospitality to care for the destitute.

- Establishing rural farming communities to teach city dwellers agrarianism and encourage a movement back-to-the-land.

- Setting up roundtable discussions in community centers in order to clarify thought and initiate action.

Maurin saw similarities between his approach and what he viewed was that of the Irish monks who evangelized medieval Europe.

Intellectual Influences

According to Dorothy Day, some of the books he had her read were the works of "Fr. Vincent McNabb and Eric Gill, Jacques Maritain, Leon Bloy, Charles Peguy of France, Don Sturzo of Italy, (Romano) Guardini of Germany, and (Nicholas) Berdyaev of Russia. Another writer upon whom Maurin drew was Emmanuel Mounier. Other titles included THE CATHOLIC CHURCH AND THE APPEAL TO REASON by Leo Paul Ward, HUMANITY'S DESTINY by Denifle, CHRISTIAN LIFE AND WORSHIP by Ellard, THE SPIRIT OF CATHOLICISM by Karl Adam, and THE SERVILE STATE by Hilaire Belloc.

The following books were recommended repeatedly by Peter Maurin in reading lists appended to his essays.

- ART IN A CHANGING CIVILIZATION, Eric Gill
- BROTHERHOOD ECONOMICS, Toyohiko Kagawa
- CHARLES V, Wyndham Lewis
- CATHOLICISM, PROTESTANTISM AND CAPITALISM, Amintore Fanfani
- THE CHURCH AND THE LAND, Father Vincent McNabb, O.P.
- DISCOURSE ON USURY, Thomas Wilson
- ENQUIRIES INTO RELIGION AND CULTURE, Christopher Dawson
- FIELDS, FACTORIES AND WORKSHOPS, Peter Kropotkin
- FIRE ON THE EARTH, Paul Hanly Furfey
- THE FLIGHT FROM THE CITY, Ralph Borsodi
- THE FRANCISCAN MESSAGE TO THE WORLD, Father Agostino Gemelli,
- FREEDOM IN THE MODERN WORLD, Jacques Maritain
- THE FUTURE OF BOLSHEVISM, Waldemar Gurian

- A GUILDSMAN'S INTERPRETATION OF HISTORY, Arthur Penty
- THE GREAT COMMANDMENT OF THE GOSPEL, His Excellency A. G. Cicognani, Apostolic Delegate to the U. S.
- IRELAND AND THE FOUNDATION OF EUROPE, Benedict Fitzpatrick
- I TAKE MY STAND, by Twelve Southern Agrarians
- THE LAND OF THE FREE, Herbert Agar
- LORD OF THE WORLD, Robert Hugh Benson
- THE MAKING OF EUROPE, Christopher Dawson
- MAN THE UNKNOWN, Dr. Alexis Carrel
- NATIONS CAN STAY AT HOME, B. O. Wilcox
- NAZARETH OR SOCIAL CHAOS, Father Vincent McNabb, O.P.
- Our Enemy the State, Albert Jay Nock
- OUTLINE OF SANITY, G. K. Chesterton
- A PHILOSOPHY OF WORK, Etienne Borne
- POST-INDUSTRIALISM, Arthur Penty
- PROGRESS AND RELIGION, Christopher Dawson
- RELIGION AND THE MODERN STATE, Christopher Dawson
- RELIGION AND THE RISE OF CAPITALISM, R. H. Tawney
- LA REVOLUTION PERSONNALISTE ET COMMUNAUTAIRE, Emmanuel Mounier
- SAINT FRANCIS OF ASSISI, G. K. Chesterton
- SOCIAL PRINCIPLES OF THE GOSPEL, Alphonse Lugan
- SOVIET MAN NOW, Helen Iswolsky
- TEMPORAL REGIME AND LIBERTY, Jacques Maritain
- THE THEORY OF THE LEISURE CLASS, Thorstein Veblen
- THOMISTIC DOCTRINE OF THE COMMON GOOD, The, Seraphine Michel
- THINGS THAT ARE NOT CAESAR'S, Jacques Maritain
- TOWARD A CHRISTIAN SOCIOLOGY, Arthur Penty
- TRUE HUMANISM, Jacques Maritain
- THE TWO NATIONS, Christopher Hollis
- THE UNFINISHED UNIVERSE, T. S. Gregory

- THE VALERIAN PERSECUTION, Father Patrick Healy
- WHAT MAN HAS MADE OF MAN, Mortimer Adler
- WORK AND LEISURE, Eric Gill

Legacy

Maurin was played by Martin Sheen in *Entertaining Angels: The Dorothy Day Story*. His contributions to the Catholic Worker Movement, while apparently often eclipsed in the collective memory of the movement by those of Dorothy Day, remain foundational, as evidenced by Day's insistence in THE LONG LONELINESS and elsewhere that she would never have begun the Catholic Worker without him. "Peter was a revelation to me," she said. [She continued:]

> *I do know this--that when people come into contact with Peter...they change, they awaken, they begin to see, things become as new, they look at life in the light of the Gospels. They admit the truth he possesses and lives by, and though they themselves fail to go the whole way, their faces are turned at least towards the light.*

APPENDIX 2

This appendix is included here because it seeks to contribute to what Peter Maurin saw as the foundational intellectual task for a new civilization that would holistically regenerate ecological, social, and spiritual life.

WASHINGTON DECLARATION

PACEM IN TERRIS GLOBAL LEADERSHIP INITIATIVE

A Humble & Prayerful Call at the End of the Modern World
for a Postmodern Global Human & Christian Renaissance
Originally issued on 19 January 2012 in Washington DC
for the Feast of Epiphany in the Eastern Churches by
Pax Romana / Catholic Movement for Intellectual & Cultural Affairs - USA
(Updated Version of 30 September 2015)

Facing the dawn of the
POSTMODERN GLOBAL ELECTRONIC-ECOLOGICAL ERA
made feasible by the Electronic Revolution,
and praying to the Holy Spirit for humility, wisdom, courage, and joy,
we invite our Catholic, Orthodox, and Protestant sisters and brothers,
including from all twenty three "sui juris" Catholic Churches,
as well as interested persons from other religions and persons of good will,
to join with us in developing the
PACEM IN TERRIS GLOBAL LEADERSHIP INITIATIVE.

This Initiative humbly and prayerfully calls for a
POSTMODERN GLOBAL HUMAN & CHRISTIAN RENAISSANCE.
This Renaissance, at once artistic, intellectual, and spiritual,
needs to promote the holistic local-global regeneration
of ecological, social and spiritual life,
in order to help us follow the life-giving way of Jesus the Christ,
and the ever-renewing inspirations of the Holy Spirit,
out of the collapsing Modern Western Industrial-Colonial Era
into the emerging Postmodern Global Electronic-Ecological Era.

In searching for this Postmodern Global Human & Christian Renaissance,
we invite people from across planet Earth to gather in faith communities,
to read the "Signs of the Times," to employ the "See-Judge-Act" method,
and to grow in vision through prayer, study, and dialogue.

The late modern erosion of life is now spreading across planet Earth
through the neo-liberal empire of financial globalization,
which is encouraging bourgeois materialist idolatries of money and power.
Those late modern bourgeois idolatries are now expanding across planet Earth
in what Saint John Paul II called an uprooting, fragmenting,
and de-spiritualizing "Culture of Death."

The late modern "Culture of Earth" is the result of deep philosophical errors
in early Modernity's underlying Epicurean materialist Cosmology.
Those errors misunderstood humans as not organically part of Nature,
They also misunderstood Nature as only mechanical.
And they misunderstood Nature as devoid of spiritual energy.
Those philosophical errors found societal expression in Western Modernity's
two materialistic ideologies of Liberal Capitalism and Scientific Socialism.

To escape from the late modern "Culture of Death,"
the Holy Spirit is calling us to discover healing paths for our human family,
whose majority now lives in the Global South of planet Earth,
so that we may all be able to navigate creatively through the "Dark Night" of
MODERN WESTERN INDUSTRIAL-COLONIAL CIVILIZATION.
toward the birthing dawn of an ecologically, spiritually, and socially regenerative
POSTMODERN GLOBAL ELECTRONIC-ECOLOGICAL CIVILIZATION.

The Holy Spirit is also calling us
to discover healing paths for our Christian family,
whose majority now also lives in the Global South of planet Earth,
so that we may be able to navigate creatively through the "Dark Night" of the
MODERN WESTERN INDUSTRIAL-COLONIAL EVANGELIZATION
toward the birthing dawn of an ecologically, spiritually, and socially regenerative
POSTMODERN GLOBAL ELECTRONIC-ECOLOGICAL EVANGELIZATION.

Through this call for a Postmodern Global Human & Christian Renaissance,
we invite faith communities across planet Earth to seek
artistic, intellectual, and spiritual grounding in four important resources:

THE BOOK OF NATURE & BOOK OF THE BIBLE,
as two complementary books of Divine revelation,
with one read though eyes of reason and the other read though eyes of faith,
with both revealing the loving Creator, Healer, & Sanctifier of the Cosmos;

THE BIBLICAL SPIRITUALITY OF CREATION,
which, according to the Eastern Christian traditions,
proclaims that all humans are "priests of creation,"
called to care for our Creator-Healer-Sanctifier's beloved human family,
and beloved ecological family of all creatures,
and to do so with joyful prayers of praise and thanksgiving;

THE POSTMODERN GLOBAL-ECOLOGICAL STAGE
OF CATHOLIC SOCIAL TEACHING,
founded by the visionary radical-traditional prophet Saint John XXIII,
enriched by Saint John's successors in the Petrine Ministry
Blessed Paul VI, John Paul I, Saint John Paul II, Benedict XVI, and now Francis,
and calling us holistically to seek global justice, peace, and ecology;

THE POSTMODERN PHILOSOPHICAL-SCIENTIFIC "NEW COSMOLOGY,"
transcending Modernity's atomizing-mechanical "Old Cosmology"
that undergirds the materialism of Liberal Capitalism and Scientific Socialism,
and perceiving a holistic, creative, and even mystical evolution,
which for postmodern Christians find its Alpha and Omega
in the loving Trinity of Creator, Healer, and Sanctifier.

Calling humbly for this
Postmodern Global Human & Christian Renaissance,
we hope and pray that the Holy Spirit
will lead those of us undertaking this Initiative
to discover healing paths for
a regenerative postmodern human way of life,
and a regenerative postmodern Christian way of life.

We seek this Postmodern Global Human & Christian Renaissance
for the sake of our children and our children's children,
and for the sake of the present and future children of all living creatures
across Earth's beauteous but threatened Biosphere.

We dedicate the search for this Renaissance to
Africa's late Kenyan ecological leader
WANGARI MAATHAI,
and to the Native-American "Lilly of the Mohawks"
SAINT KATERI TEKAWITHA,
As well as to all visionary young people
who seek locally and globally to regenerate
the creative communion of ecological, social, and spiritual life.

Finally, we ask for constant prayer that
the Holy Spirit guide those of us seeking this Renaissance,
as together we seek a regenerative postmodern global future
for our global Christian family, our global human family,
and our global ecological family,
and as we all dwell together within the vibrant community of life
across our Creator-Healer-Sanctifier's beloved garden-planet Earth.

BOOKS FROM PACEM IN TERRIS PRESS

Toward a Regenerative Postmodern Global Ecological Civilization
and a Regenerative Postmodern Ecological World Church

CATHOLIC LABOR PRIESTS
Five Giants in the United States Catholic Bishops Social Action Department
Volume I of US Labor Priests During the 20th Century
Patrick Sullivan, 2014

CATHOLIC SOCIAL TEACHING & UNIONS
IN CATHOLIC PRIMARY & SECONDARY SCHOOLS
The Clash between Theory & Practice within the United States
Walter "Bob" Baker, 2014

SPIRITUAL PATHS TO
A GLOBAL & ECOLOGICAL CIVILIZATION
Reading the Signs of the Times with Buddhists, Christians, & Muslims
John Raymaker & Gerald Grudzen, with Joe Holland, 2013

PACEM IN TERRIS
Its Continuing Relevance for the Twenty-First Century
(Papers from the 50th Anniversary Conference at the United Nations)
Josef Klee & Francis Dubois, Editors, 2013

PACEM IN TERRIS
Summary & Commentary for the Famous Encyclical Letter
of Pope John XXIII on World Peace
Joe Holland, 2012

100 YEARS OF CATHOLIC SOCIAL TEACHING
DEFENDING WORKERS & THEIR UNIONS
Summaries & Commentaries for Five Landmark Papal Encyclicals
Joe Holland, 2012

HUMANITY'S AFRICAN ROOTS
Remembering the Ancestors' Wisdom
Joe Holland, 2012

THE "POISONED SPRING" OF ECONOMIC LIBERTARIANISM
Menger, Mises, Hayek, Rothbard: A Critique from
Catholic Social Teaching of the Austrian School of Economics
Pax Romana / Cmica-usa
Angus Sibley, 2011

BEYOND THE DEATH PENALTY
The Development in Catholic Social Teaching
Florida Council of Catholic Scholarship
D. Michael McCarron & Joe Holland, Editors, 2007

THE NEW DIALOGUE OF CIVILIZATIONS
A Contribution from Pax Romana
International Catholic Movement for Intellectual & Cultural Affairs
Pax Romana / Cmica-usa
Roza Pati & Joe Holland, Editors, 2002

Forthcoming soon from Pacem in Terris Press

THOMAS BERRY IN ITALY
Reflections on Spirituality & Sustainability
Elisabeth Ferrero, Editor, Forthcoming in 2015

TOWARD THE DAWN OF
POSTMODERN CATHOLIC ECOLOGICAL SPIRITUALITY
The Twilight of Modern Psychological Spirituality,
the Dark Night of Modern Industrial-Colonial Civilization, and
Peter Maurin's Call for a New Lay Monasticism
Joe Holland, Forthcoming in 2015

SOCIAL ANALYSIS II
END OF THE MODERN WORLD
Toward a Regenerative Postmodern Global Ecological Civilization
Joe Holland, Forthcoming in 2016

REMEMBERING THE
PROPHETIC VISION OF ST. JOHN XXIII
Radical Traditional Founder of
Postmodern Global-Ecological Catholic Social Teaching
Joe Holland, Forthcoming in 2016

ADDITIONAL BOOKS BY JOE HOLLAND

(In Addition to his books published by Pacem in Terris Press)

MODERN CATHOLIC SOCIAL TEACHING 1740-1958
The Popes Confront the Industrial Age
Paulist Press, 2003

"THE EARTH CHARTER"
A Study Book of Reflection for Action
Co-Author Elisabeth Ferrero
Redwoods Press, 2002
(also in Italian & Portuguese versions)

VARIETIES OF POSTMODERN THEOLOGY
Co-Editors David Griffin & William Beardslee,
State University of New York Press, 1989

CREATIVE COMMUNION
Toward a Spirituality of Work
Paulist Press, 1989

AMERICAN AND CATHOLIC
The New Debate
Co-Editor Anne Barsanti
Pillar Books, 1988

VOCATION AND MISSION OF THE LAITY
Co-Author Robert Maxwell
Pillar Books, 1986

SOCIAL ANALYSIS
Linking Faith and Justice
Co-Author Peter J. Henriot SJ
Orbis Books, 1980 & 1983
(with many foreign language versions)

THE AMERICAN JOURNEY
A Theology in the Americas Working Paper
IDOC, 1976

ABOUT THE AUTHOR

JOE HOLLAND, a philosopher and Catholic theologian, advocates a postmodern ecological-humanistic global civilization. He received his Ph.D. from the University of Chicago in the field of Ethics & Society, an interdisciplinary dialogue among Philosophy, Social Science, and Theology. At Chicago, he studied Social Science with Gibson Winter, Theology with David Tracy, and Philosophy with Paul Ricoeur. He was also a Fulbright Scholar in Philosophy at the Universidad Católica in Santiago, Chile.

Currently, Joe serves as: Professor of Philosophy & Religion, as well as Adjunct Professor in the School of Law and in the School of Theology & Ministry, at Saint Thomas University in Miami Gardens, Florida; Permanent Visiting Professor at the Universidad Nacional del Altiplano, Puno, Peru; President of Pax Romana / Catholic Movement for Intellectual & Cultural Affairs USA, Washington DC; Vice-Chair of Catholic Scholars for Worker Justice, Boston, Massachusetts; and a member of the International Association for Catholic Social Thought, based at the Catholic University of Leuven in Belgium.

Earlier, Joe served as an Associate at the Washington DC Center of Concern, created jointly by the international Jesuits and the US Catholic Bishops to work with the United Nations on global social issues. At the Center, he co-founded the National Conference on Religion & Labor, sponsored by the AFL-CIO, and the American Catholic Lay Network. He also served as founding Director of the Pallottine Institute for Lay Leadership & Research at Seton Hall University in New Jersey, and he co-founded Catholic Scholars for Worker Justice.

Joe has published 15 books and many articles. His SOCIAL ANALYSIS book with Peter Henriot SJ has over 100,000 copies in print, with more than 20 US printings plus 5 foreign-language translations and 2 foreign English editions. He was also the consultant-writer for the 1975 document THIS LAND IS HOME TO ME, *a Pastoral Letter on Powerlessness in Appalachia by the Catholic Bishops of the Region*, and for the 1995 sequel document AT HOME IN THE WEB OF LIFE, *a Pastoral Message from the Catholic Bishops of Appalachia on Sustainable Communities*.

In the United States, Joe has lectured at Georgetown, Harvard, Notre Dame, Princeton, and other universities. Internationally, he has lectured at Institut Catholique in Paris, France; Sophia University in Tokyo, Japan; Pontifical Catholic University in São Paulo, Brazil; Pontifical Catholic University in Porto Alegre, Brazil; Universidad Mayor de San Andres in La Paz, Bolivia; and Universidad Nacional del Altiplano in Puno, Peru. In 1986, he received the Isaac Hecker Award for Social Justice; in 2002, the Athena Medal of Excellence from the Universidad Nacional del Altiplano; and in 2013, the Irish Echo's "Labor 100" award for his contribution to the US labor movement.

Joe is married to the Paquita Biascoechea-Martinez Holland, and they have two children and four grandchildren.

This booklet and the larger book
from which it has been excerpted and adapted
are available from:

www.amazon.com/books

For more information on the
Pacem in Terris Global Leadership Initiative
please go to:

www.paceminterris.net

www.ingramcontent.com/pod-product-compliance
Lightning Source LLC
Chambersburg PA
CBHW060631030426
42337CB00018B/3303